REVEAL ART ANIMALS

SparkPool

MASTERING STIPPLE ART

'Stippling' is an art technique that forms a pattern or picture by filling in dots. Anyone can create wonderful artwork using this method – tighter-packed dots create a deeper shading effect, whereas larger and more sporadic dots give a lighter effect. Use a single colour – a fine pointed pen or pencil works best – to complete the areas or dots and watch as the page transforms into an incredible design.

- If you are using a pen, test this out first on a separate piece of paper. Try to select a pen which does not bleed and has a small tip, for expert precision.
- Keep your eyes peeled for when the clustered areas change to complete circles – sometimes this can be tricky to spot and you will have to adjust your technique from colouring outside the dots to inside them!
- If you are looking for guidance on whether you are completing the page correctly, start colouring from the prompt on each page, or have a peek at the completed designs at the back of the book.

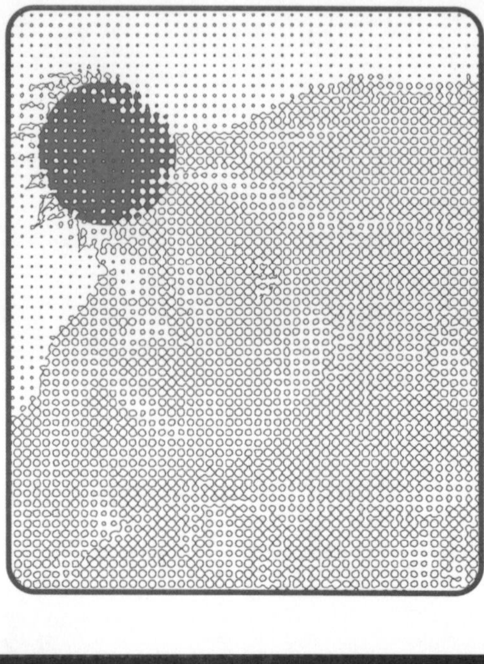

HELPFUL DOT ART TIPS

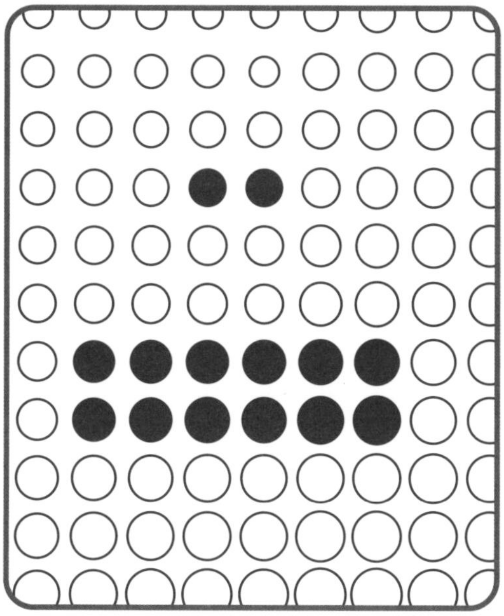

Whole dots

Where you find areas of complete, round dots which do not merge with anything around them, fill these in with your pen or pencil.

Cluster dots

Where you find an area where the circles merge together to create a larger, enclosed area, fill the area with your pen or pencil, leaving the smaller spaces and dots blank.

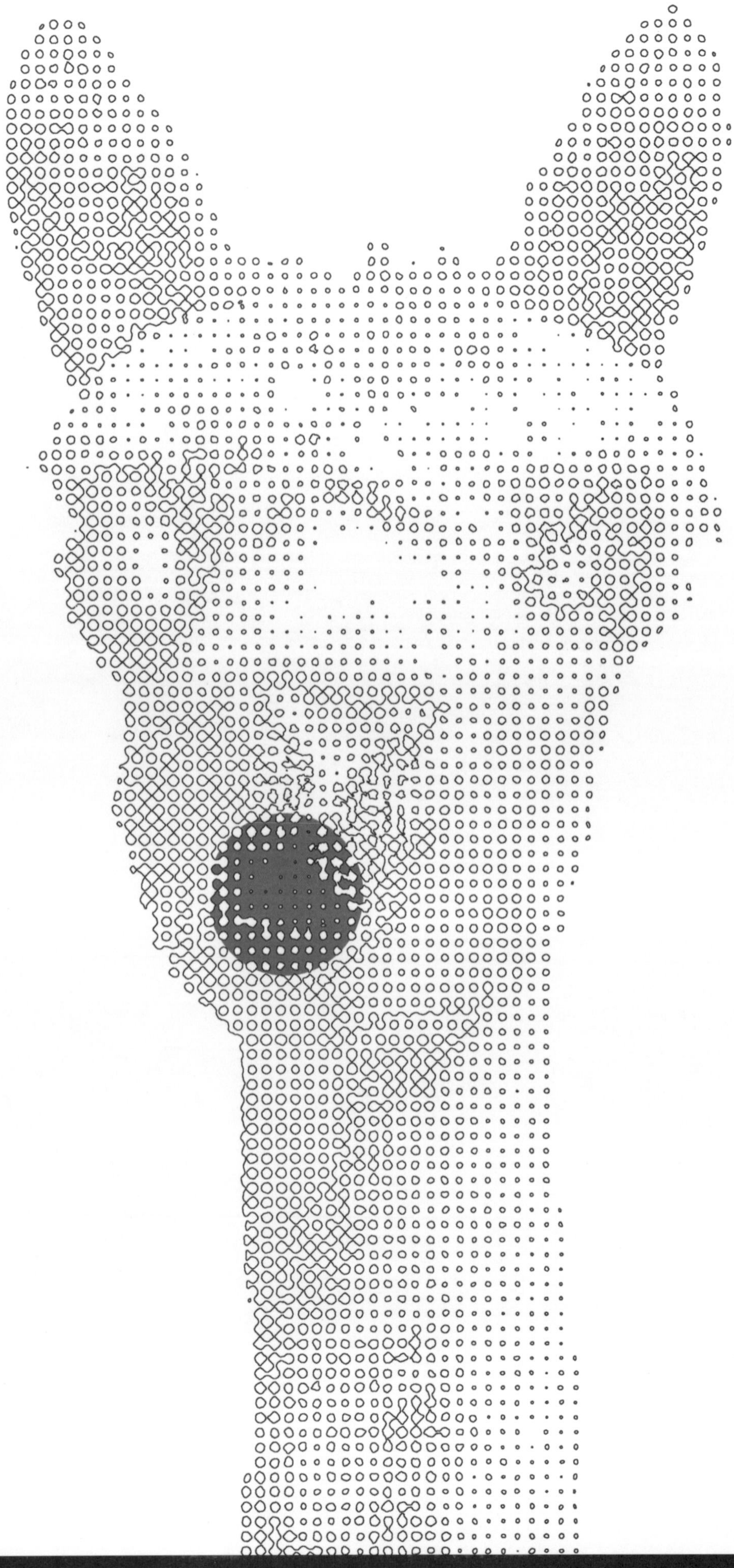

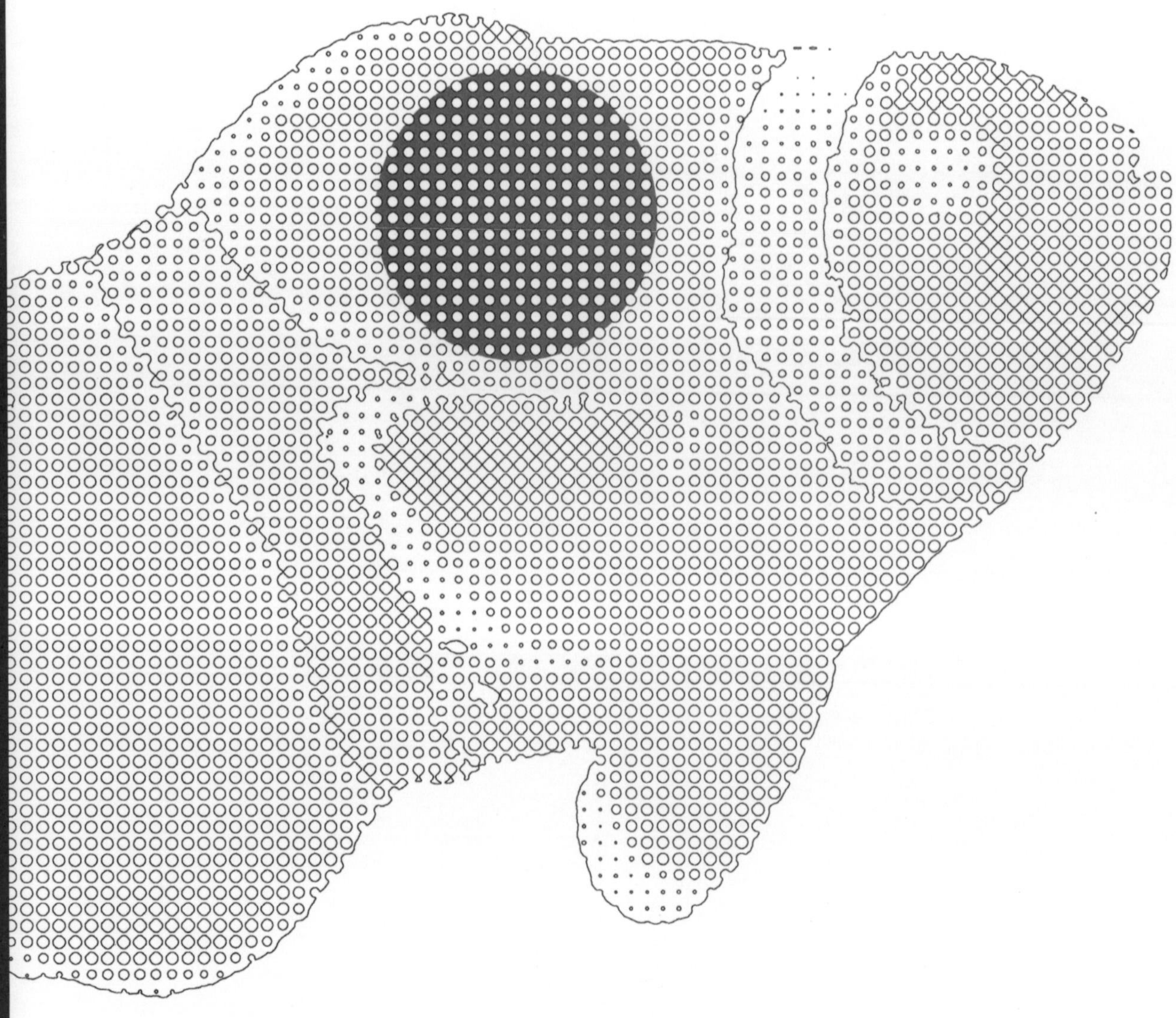

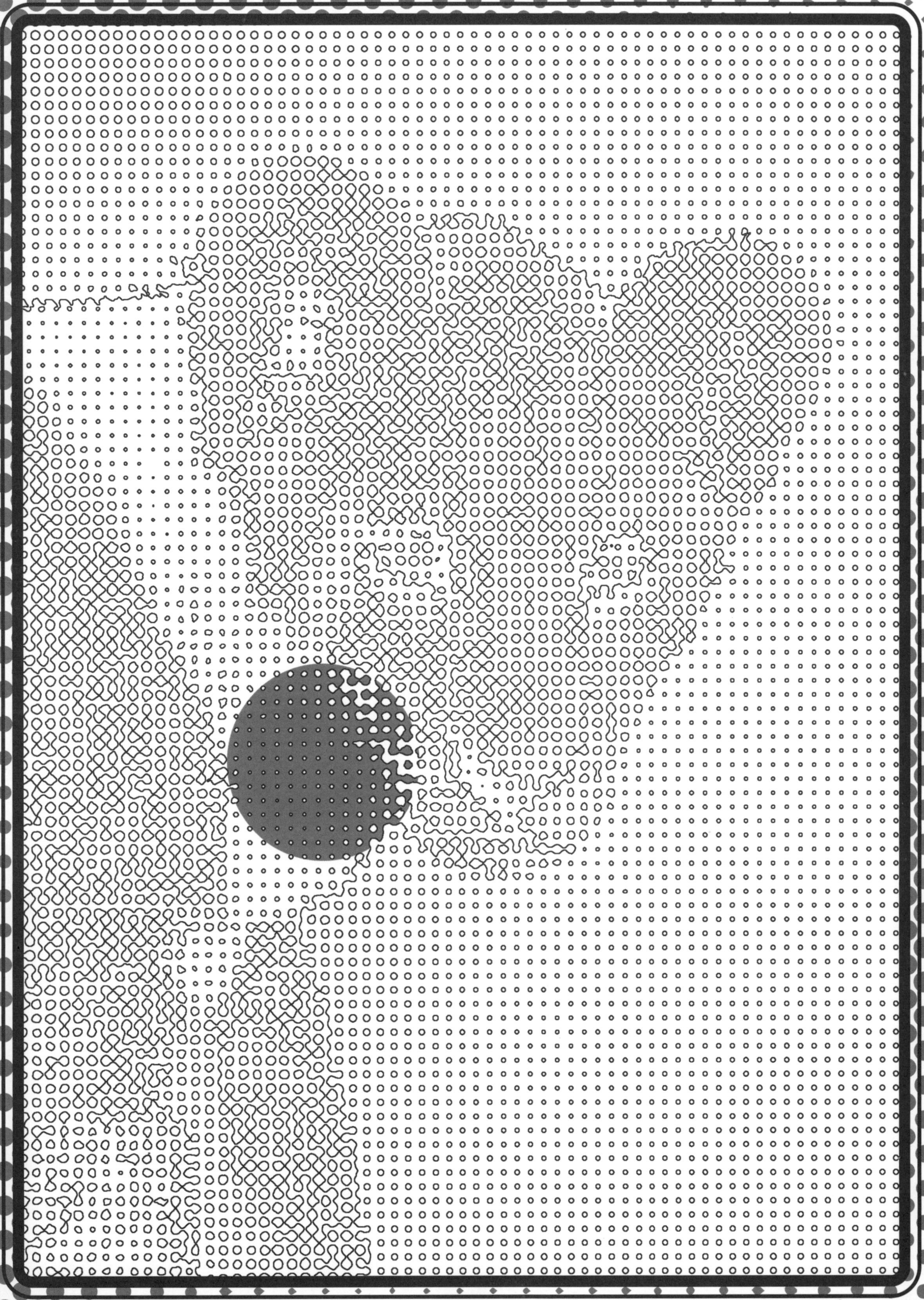

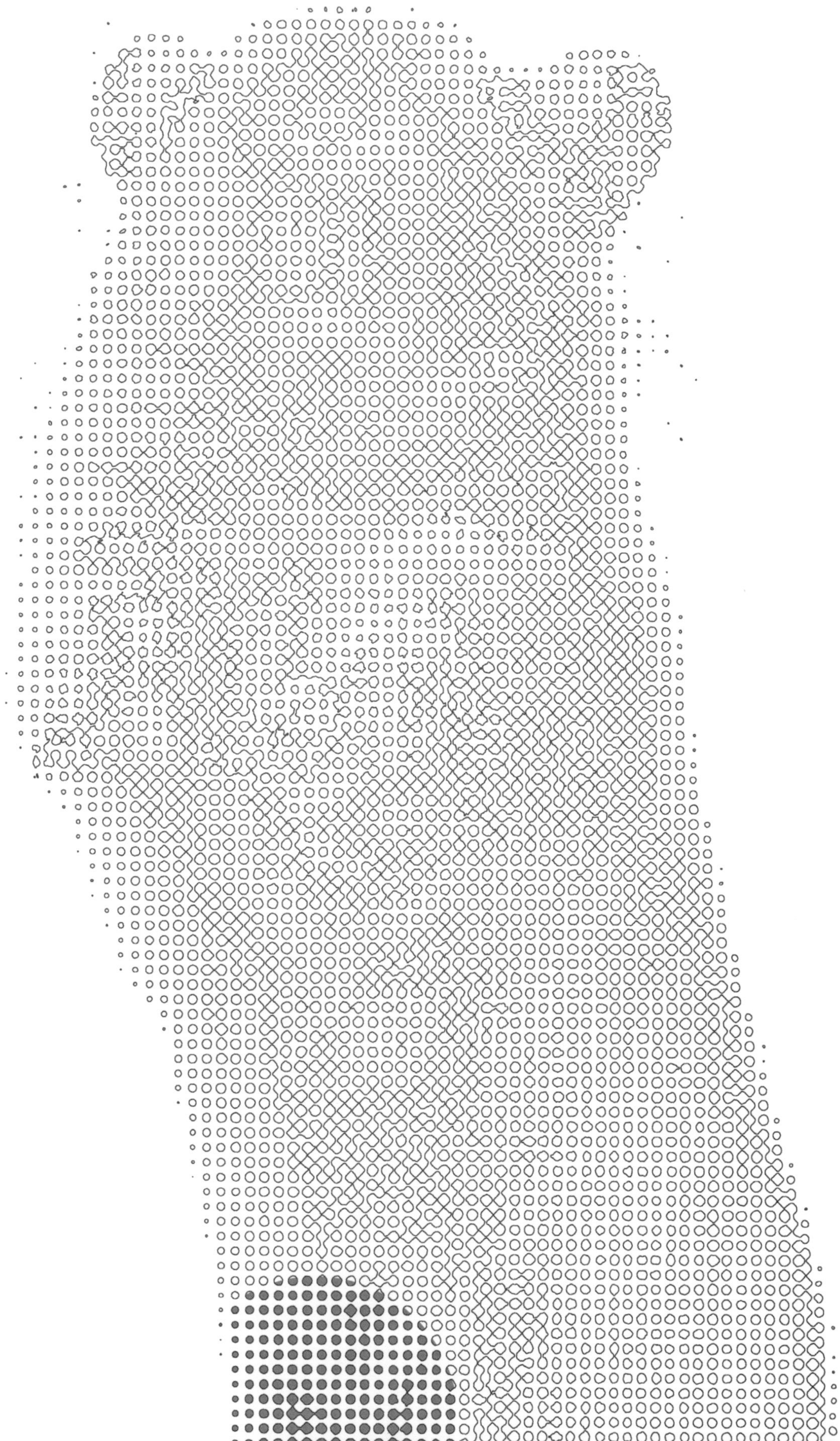

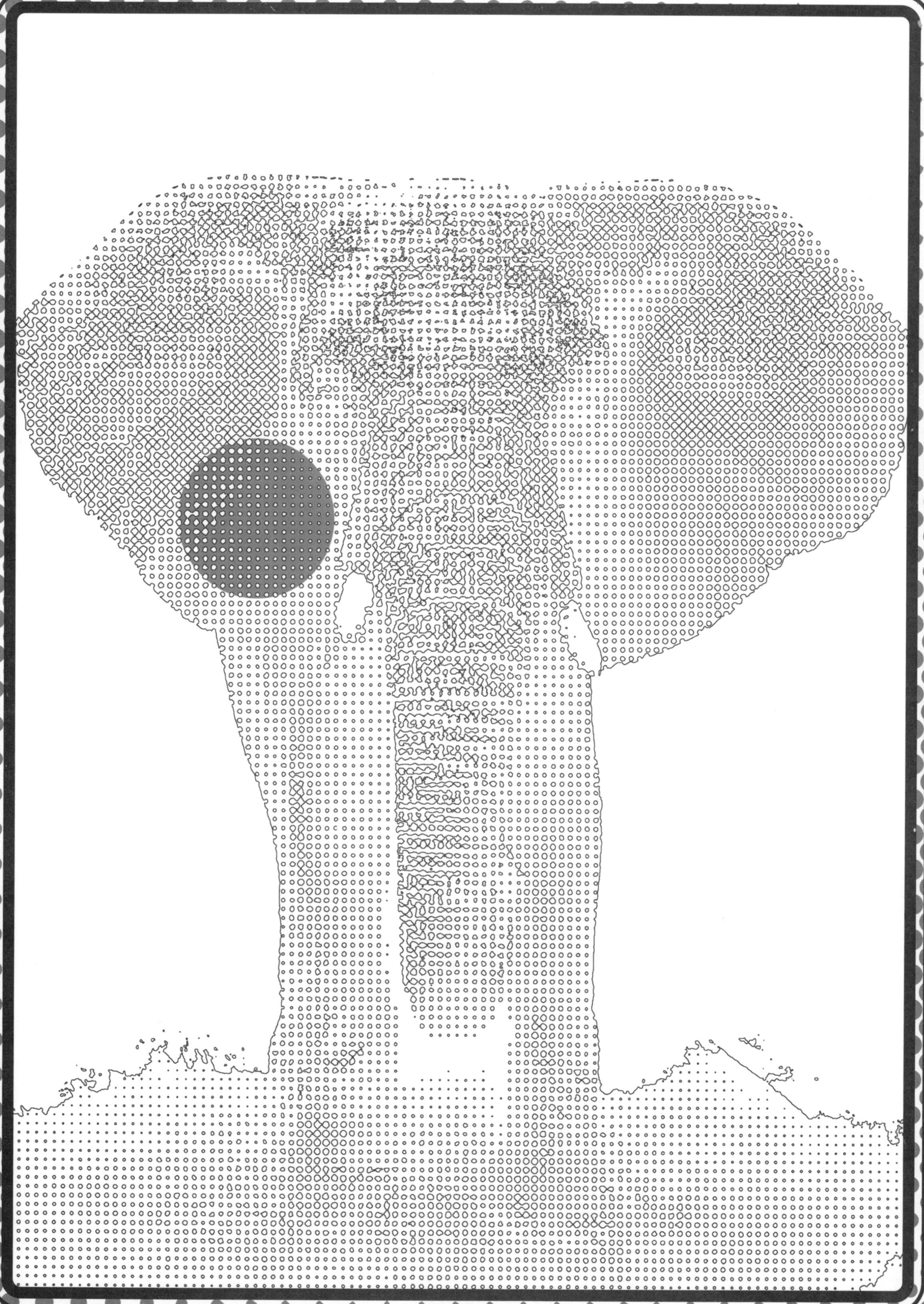

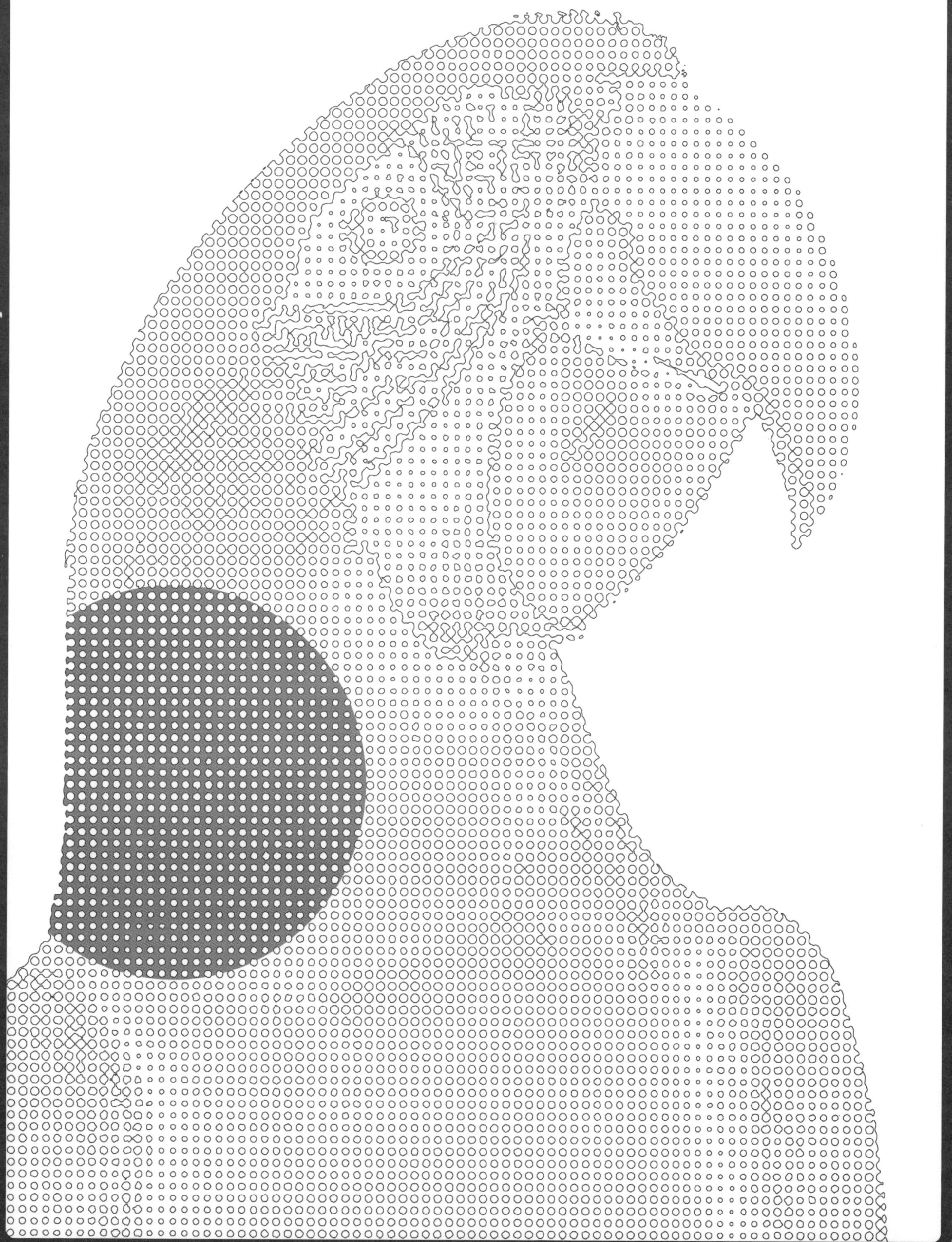

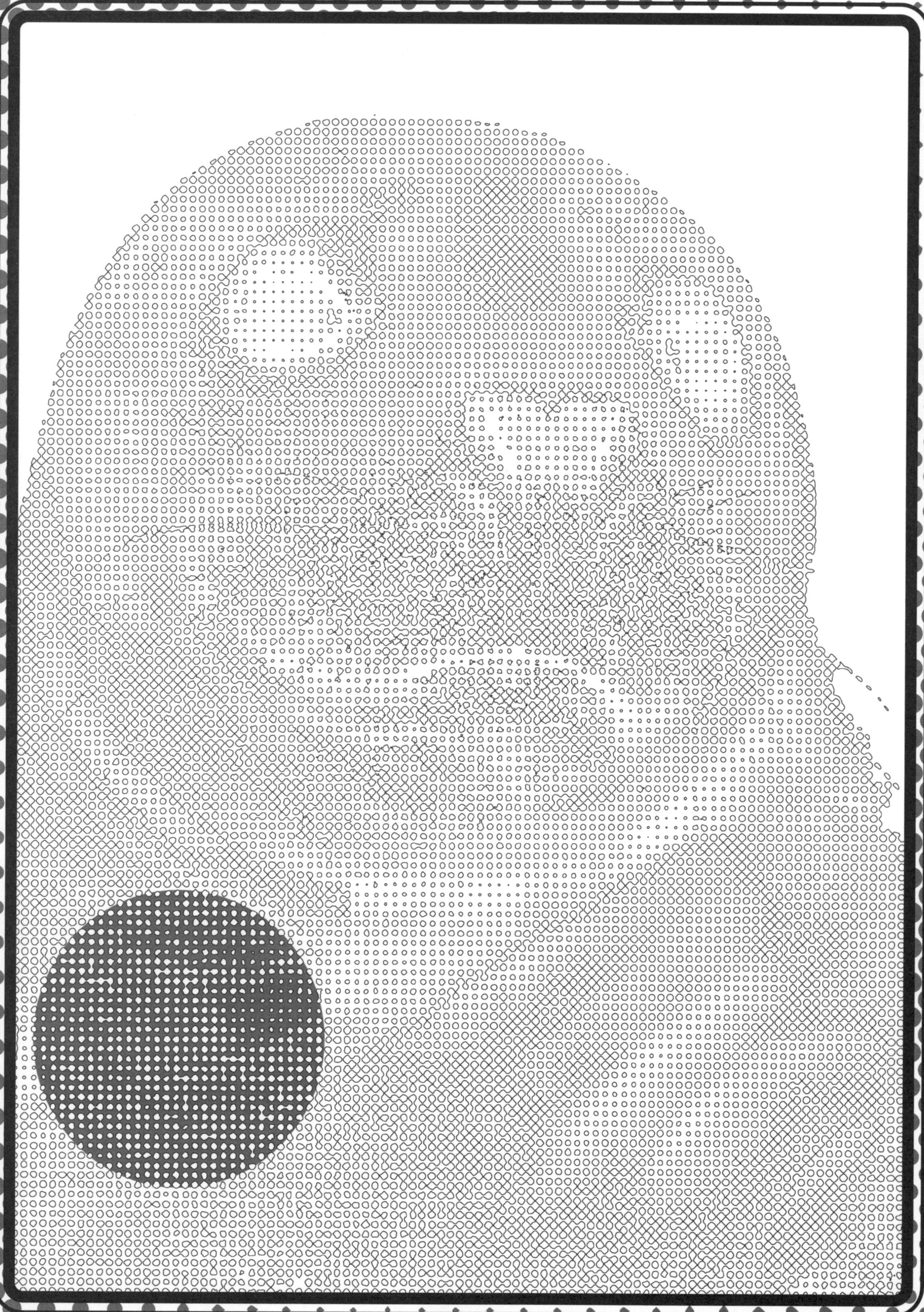

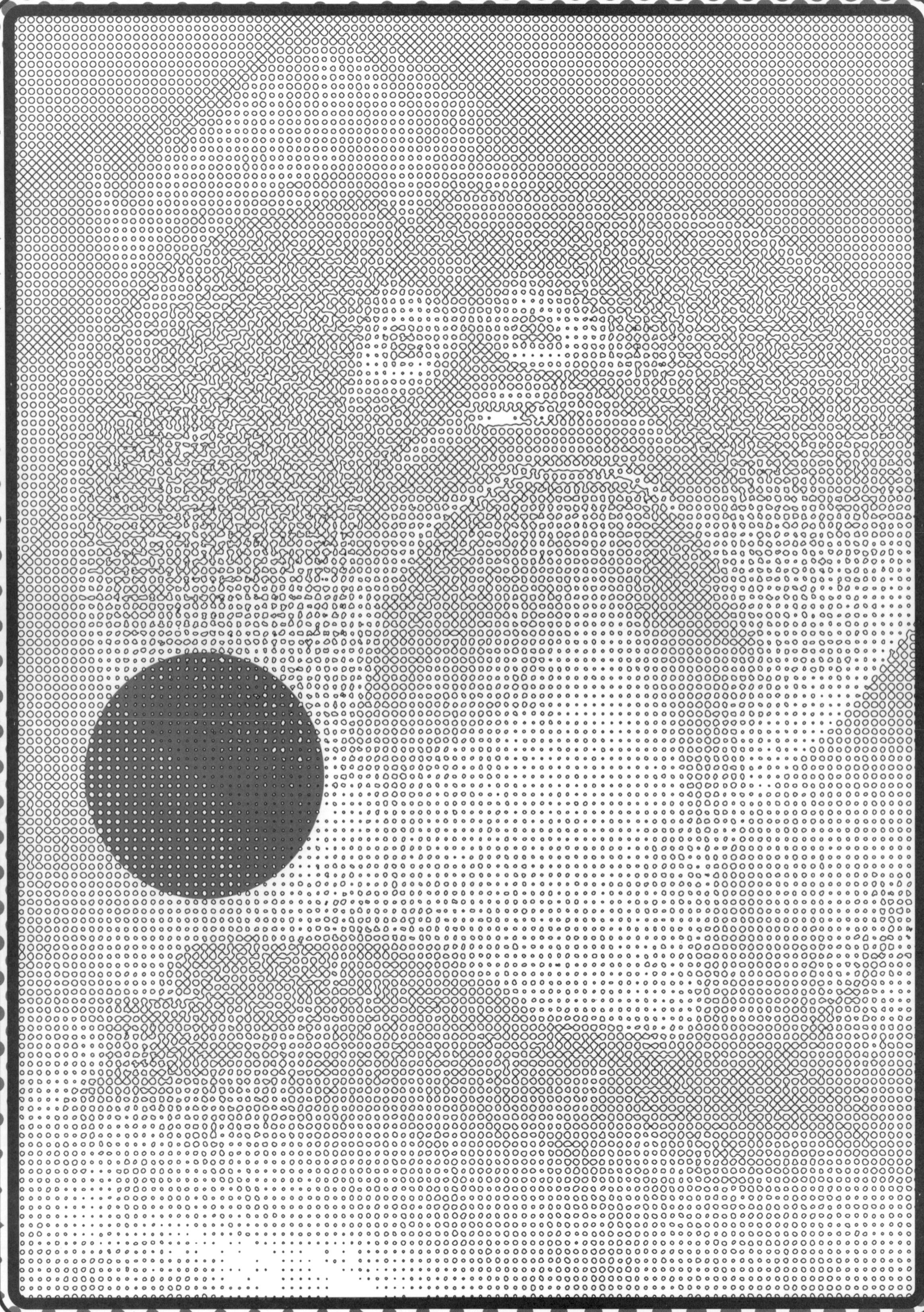

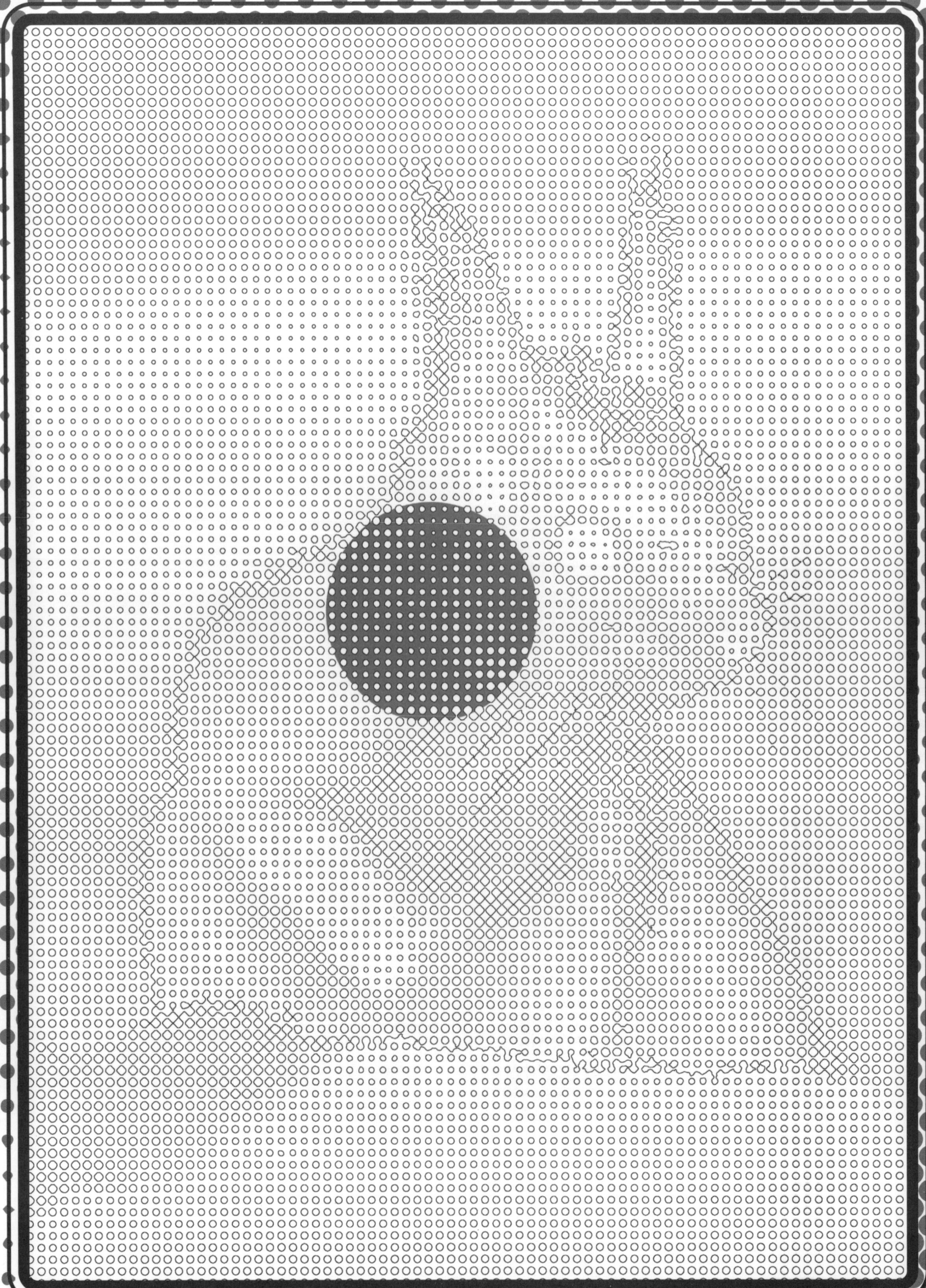

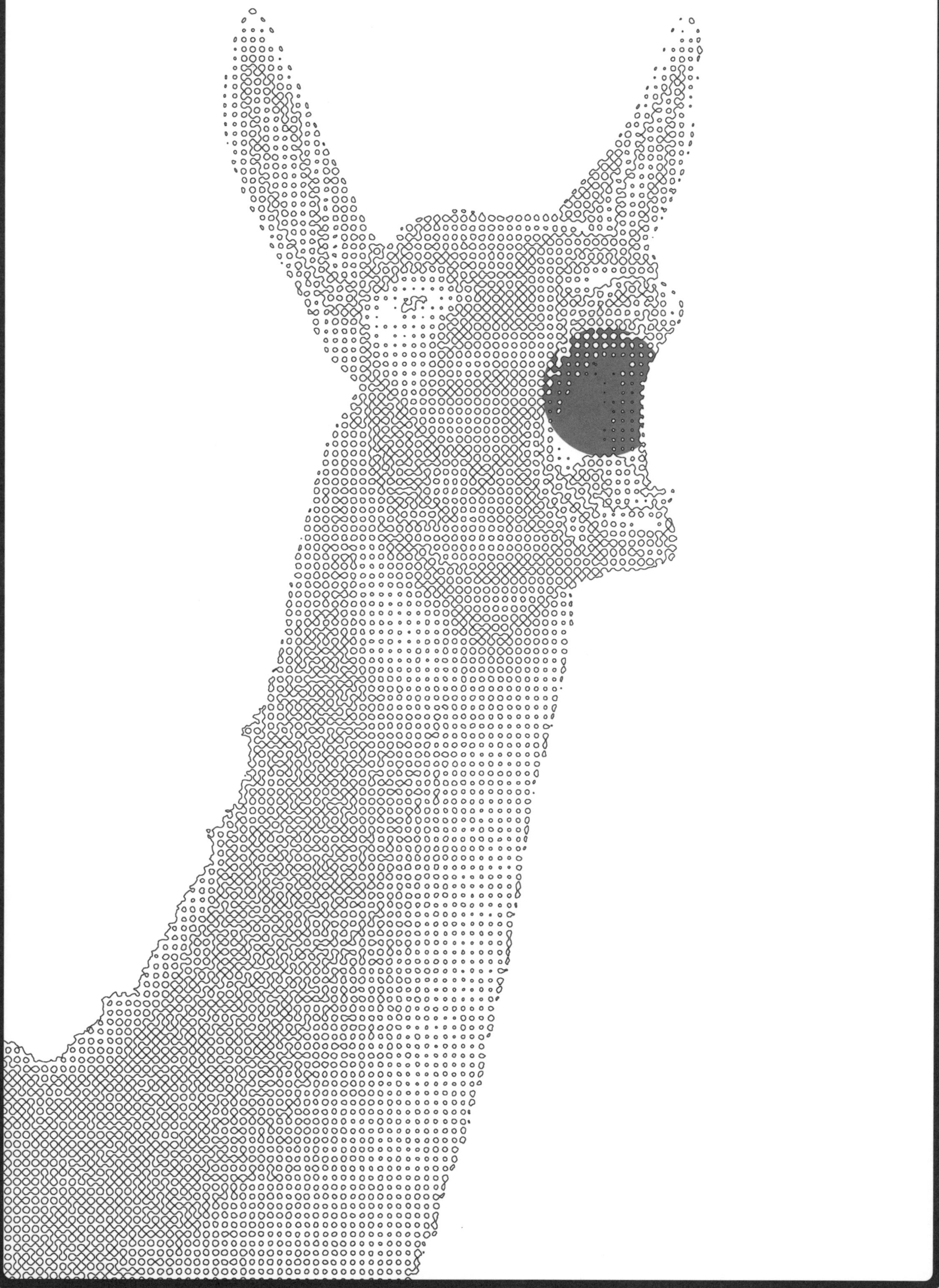

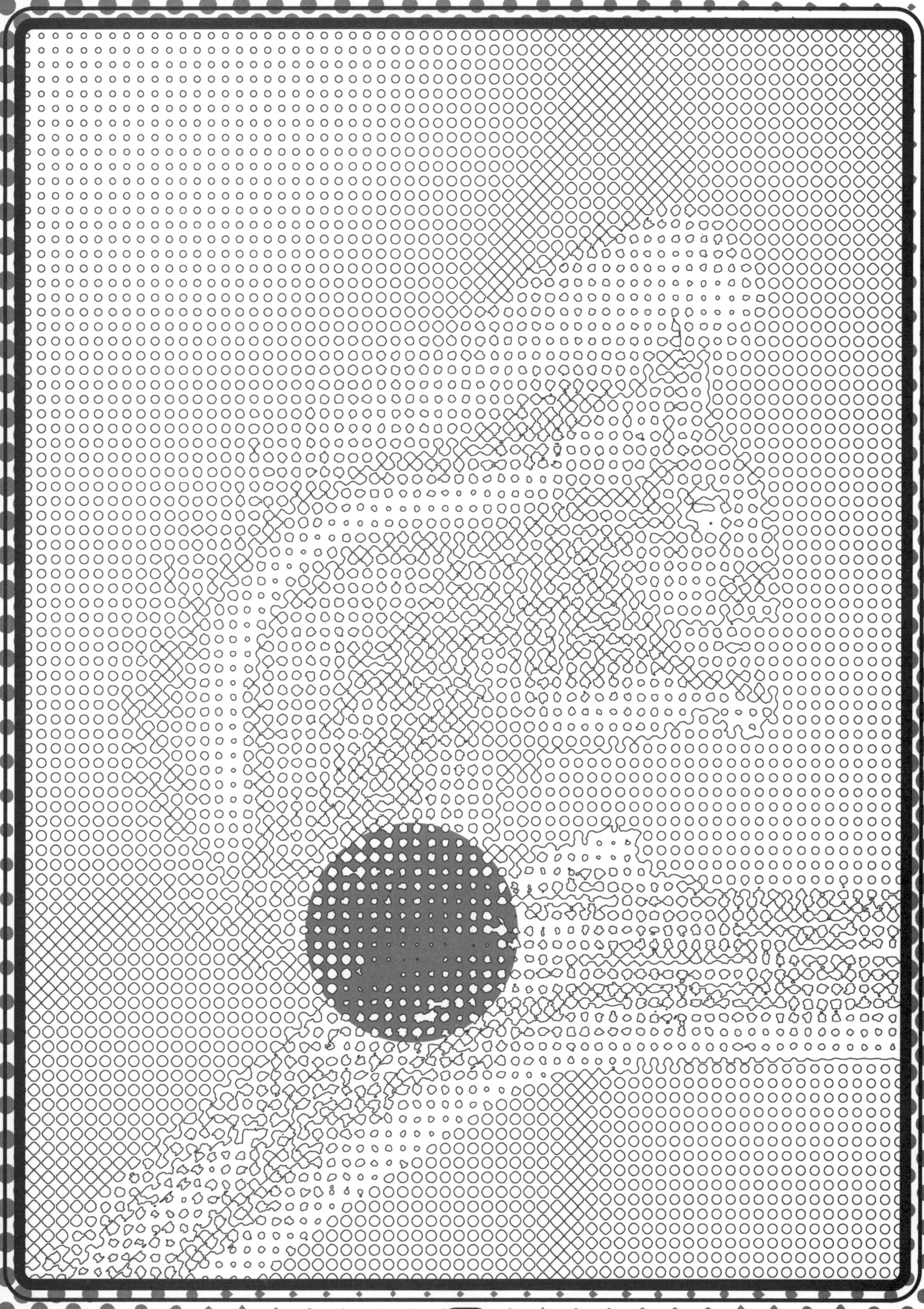

SOLUTIONS

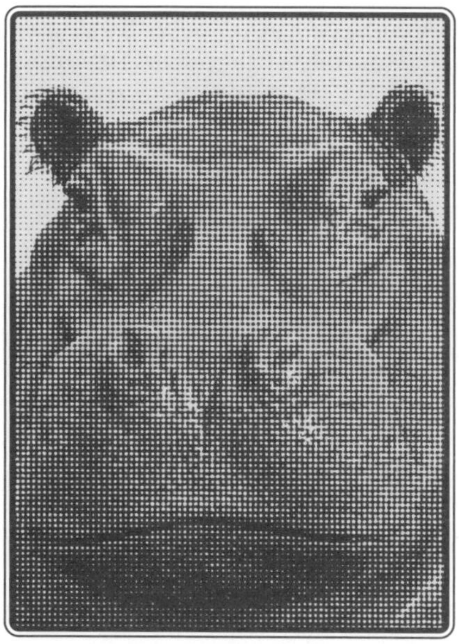

1

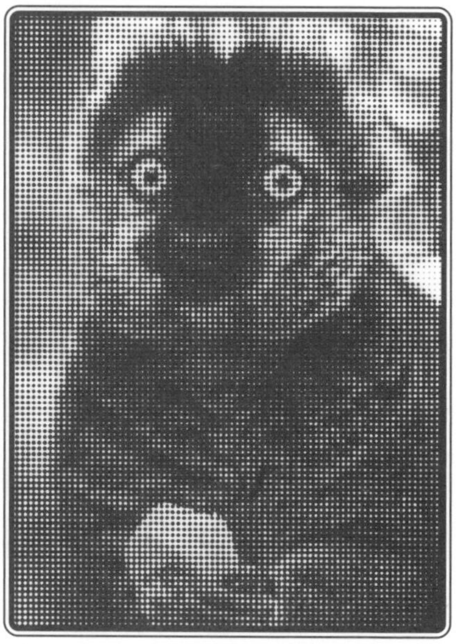

2

3

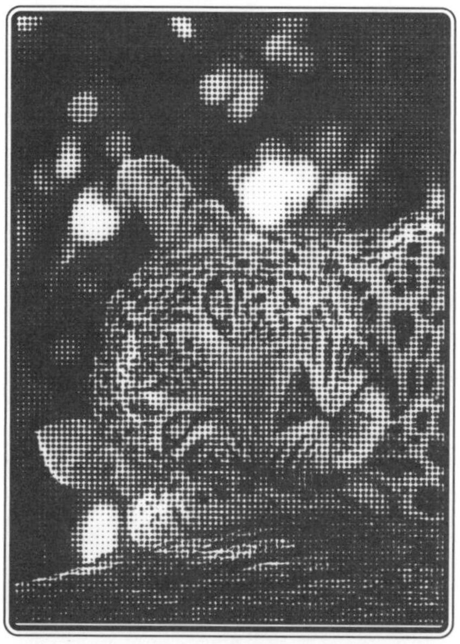

4

5

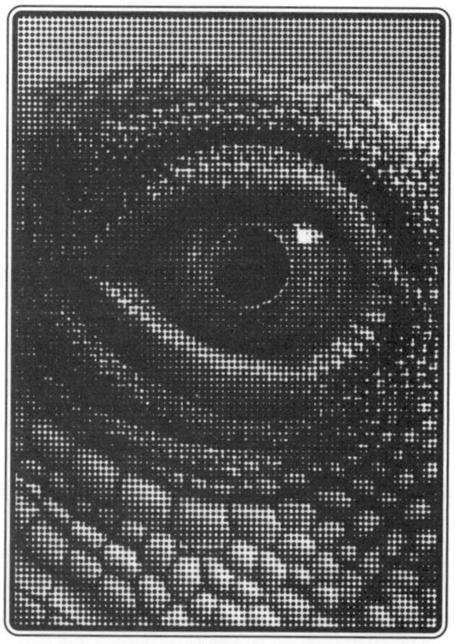

6

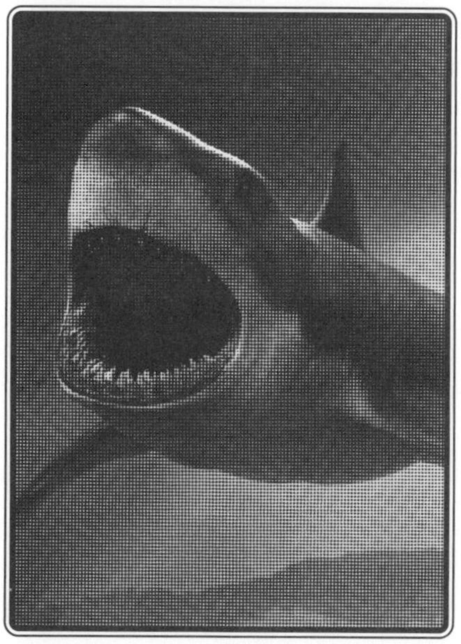

7

8

9

SOLUTIONS

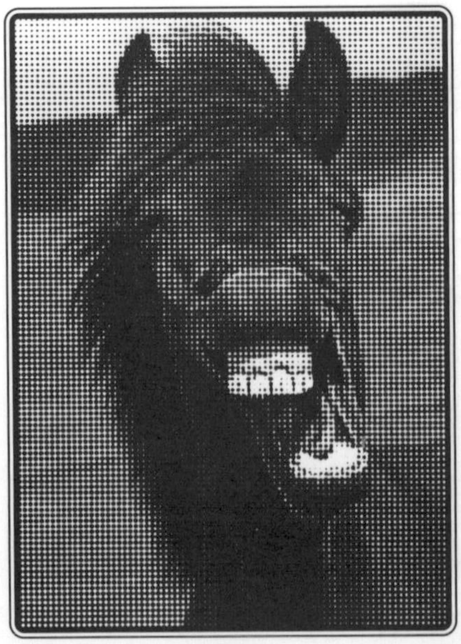

10

11

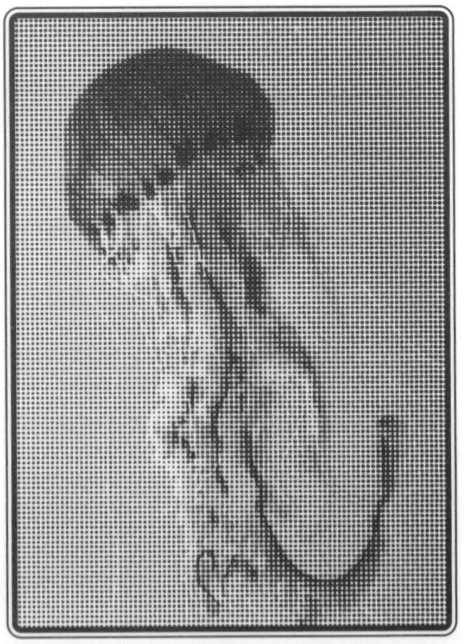

12

13

14

15

16

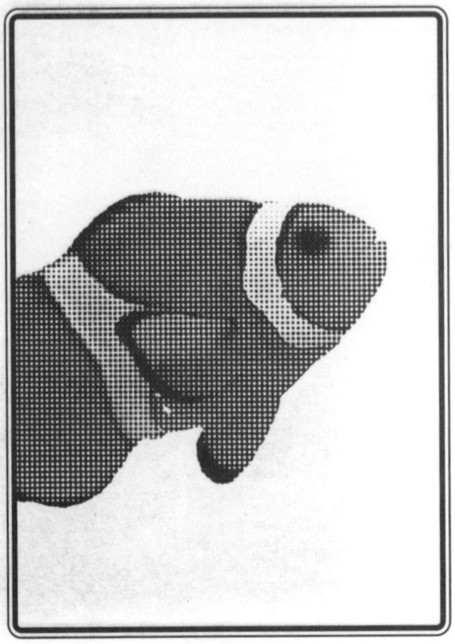

17

18

SOLUTIONS

19

20

21

22

23

24

25

26

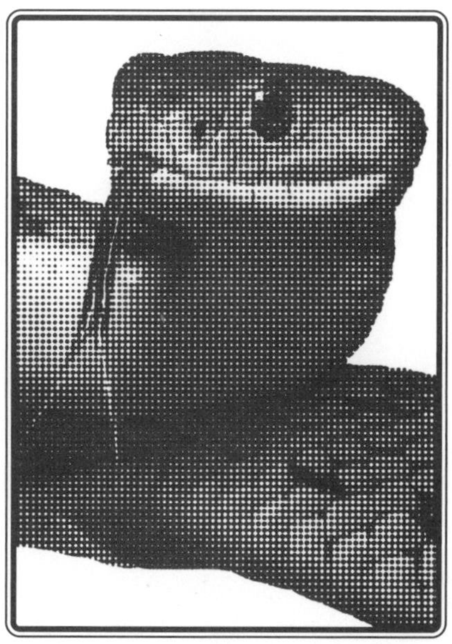

27

SOLUTIONS

28

29

30

31

32

33

34

35

36

37

38

39

SOLUTIONS

40

41

42

43

44

45

46

47

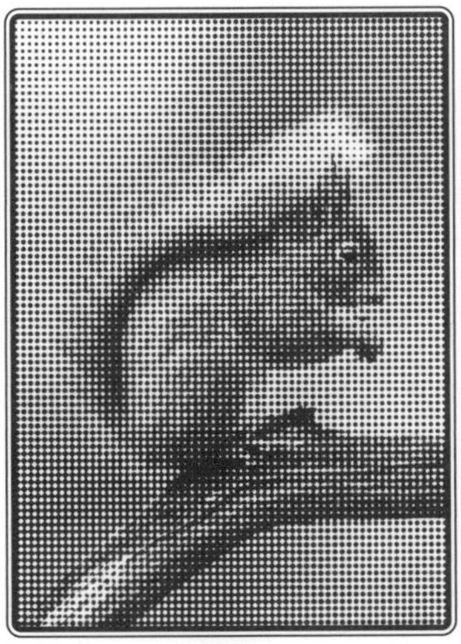
48

49

50

51